Do Life Different

Jill Hart

© 2014/2017 by Jill Hart

ISBN 978-1-943027-04-0

All rights reserved. No part of this publication may be reproduced or transmitted for commercial purposes, except for brief quotations in printed or electronic reviews, without written permission of the publisher. Churches and other noncommercial interests may reproduce portions of this book not to exceed 500 words or five percent of the book without the express written permission of Electric Moon Publishing, LLC, provided that the text is not material quoted from another publisher. When reproducing text from this book, include the following credit line: "From *Do Life Different*, written by Jill Hart, published by Electric Moon Publishing, LLC. Used by permission."

Printed in the United States of America.

All Scripture references are taken from the New International Version (NIV) except where otherwise noted. Used by permission.

Videos corresponding to each devotion are available at www.dolifedifferent.org. They are the property of Jill Hart and are made available for use in conjunction with this book.

All rights reserved worldwide.

Do Life Different

Inspiring Powerful Living

Jill Hart

www.cwahm.com
www.dolifedifferent.org
www.emoonpublishing.com

Endorsements

"In Jill Hart's new devotional, she helps women press the pause button and be refreshed with the Word of God and encouragement from another mom whose been there. Her sweet style will make you feel like someone just handed you a latte and gave you a mid-morning break! You'll be inspired to keep sight of what's really important and thrive in your calling to work from home."

Glynnis Whitwer ~ Author of I Used to Be So Organized, Executive Director of Communications, Proverbs 31 Ministries (working from home)

"Do Life Different! Take the challenge! Be the woman God made you to be. Think you can't live up to the Proverbs 31 woman? Think again. DO LIFE DIFFERENT will not only make you see how special you are, it will comfort and encourage you and help reveal the lustrous pearl God has hidden within your heart."

MaryLu Tyndall ~ author of the Escape to Paradise series

Jill Hart

"As a mother of three, wife, friend, chauffeur, business owner, dishwasher and an endless list of other titles, I fully understand the juggling act we all face. What a winner Jill Hart has in her new book *Do Life Different*! With more than a decade of Work-At-Home expertise, Jill Hart offers you much-needed guidance, support, and encouragement."

> *Jennifer Maggio ~ CEO of The Life of a Single Mom Ministries and author*

"Finally a devotional specifically for the work-at-home mom. You'll be blessed by Jill's insight and wisdom as she delves into God's Word with powerful teaching, and then challenges you to apply it. A fabulous tool to help us stay focused on His purposes in our lives and in our roles as wife and mother."

> *Lesley Pyle, MSc. ~ HBWM.com Inc.*
> *HomeBasedWorkingMoms.com, HireMyMom.com*

"Jill Hart is a terrific leader whose walk matches her talk. I love the honest and easy style with which she writes. Energy, excitement, honesty and integrity are words that describe the pages of Do Life Different. Read this book and enjoy life more than ever!"

> *Dr. Stan Toler ~ Bestselling Author & Speaker*

Do Life Different

"In brief, easy-to-understand devotionals, Jill helps us connect to the Bible and to God's plan for our lives. The passages she shares are simple, but the insight is practical and profound! I highly recommend this positive, empowering, and deeply spiritual book."

Rev. Brad Washburn CHT, CPC ~ Clinical Director at PathSeeker Center

"Jill Hart challenges all work-at-home moms to truly *Do Life Different*. Her devotion is a breath a fresh air covering topics which every work-a- home or even stay-at-home battles. This devotion speaks the language and heart of God's grace, love and tender mercy. It's time to start DOING and not just existing. This devotion is a great starting off point to living the life Christ has called all His daughters of purpose to."

Roshanda E. Pratt ~ marketing strategist and media curator at R.E.P Communications Network

"Jill Hart acts as a Bible study partner and companion, sharing great truths and insightful challenges to guide the stay-at-home mom to a deeper relationship with Jesus."

Bonnie S. Calhoun ~ Publisher at Christian Fiction Online Magazine and author of Pieces of the Heart

Contents

1. NO MORE EXCUSES	15
2. A WOMAN OF NOBLE CHARACTER	18
3. FULL CONFIDENCE	21
4. EAGER	24
5. THE JOY OF THE MORNING	27
6. MAKING WISE DECISIONS	30
7. GOD'S ECONOMY	33
8. OVERCOMING FEAR AND WORRY	36
9. SEEKING WISDOM	39
10. STRIVING TO PLEASE GOD	42
11. PURSUING EXCELLENCE WHEN WE FEEL MEDIOCRE	45
12. THE BALANCING ACT	48
13. BUSINESS AS MINISTRY	51
14. TAKING STEPS OF FAITH	54
15. STARTING FRESH	57
16. DON'T HIDE FROM YOUR CALLING	60
17. I'LL HANDLE THIS	63
18. FULFILL YOUR CALLING	66
19. DO THE WORK	69
20. IT'S A CHOICE	72
21. YOUR RESPONSE COUNTS	75
22. SERVING GOD NOT PEOPLE	78
23. ENJOY YOUR WORK	81
24. DOES YOUR BUSINESS SHOUT?	83
25. SOMETIMES YOU GOTTA GO FOR IT	86
26. THE SMALLEST THING	89

27. BETTER LATE THAN NEVER	92
28. WHAT WILL YOU CHOOSE?	95
29. THE GOD WHO WASTES NOTHING	98
30. GOD USES NOBODIES	101
31. WHAT IF GOD HAS BIGGER PLANS FOR YOU?	104
32. FINDING YOUR HIDDEN TALENTS	107
33. DOING IT GOD'S WAY	110
34. WHEN WE ARE WEAK	113
35. FEELING RESTLESS	116
36. MADE FOR A SPECIAL PURPOSE	119
37. WHEN WE ARE STRUGGLING	122
38. LIVING IN ABUNDANCE	125
39. WORKING THROUGH THE IMPOSSIBLE	128
40. SEEING THE LEADER WITHIN	131
41. IS SUCCESS OKAY?	134
42. HOW TO BALANCE IT ALL	137
43. WHAT'S YOUR GOAL?	140
44. GET OFF YOUR DUFF	143
45. THE ACT OF STARTING	146
46. ALL TALK	149
47. APPEARANCES	152
48. CHOOSING JOY	155
49. ARE YOU USING WHAT GOD HAS GIVEN YOU?	158
50. SUCCESS WITHOUT PAIN?	161
51. THAT PESKY STEP OF FAITH	164
52. MAKE YOUR LIFE COUNT	167

Preface

Welcome, work-at-home mom! I'm so glad you've decided to dive into this book and learn some ways to *Do Life Different*. Perhaps you've chosen to work from home to answer the needs of your family, to make yourself more available for opportunity, or to have more personal flexibility. Whatever your reason, you've no doubt found that, like all journeys, the one of the work-at-home mom bears its own set of challenges.

These devotions are truly written from my heart to yours. Each day's writing is taken from lessons God has taught (and is teaching) me during my quiet times with Him. I may not be able to answer the specifics of your individual concerns, but I can help you dig into scripture and find out what God says about them.

When my kids were small and still at home with me all day every day, I kept a copy of a devotional in the bathroom. It was the only place where I might be lucky enough to have two minutes to myself to read, savor, and ponder what God might have for me that day. I would carry those words around and meditate on what God had said to me the rest of the day. His

Jill Hart

Word carried me through those wonderful but exhausting years.

We've included 52 devotions. That's just one per week. So, if you're like me and struggle to find time to get deep in God's Word I pray that these will help make it just a bit easier for you. And if you do use this as a weekly devotional, I would encourage you to also pick a book of the Bible (Proverbs is a great place to start) and read a verse daily.

Also, if you visit www.emoonpublishing.com or www.cwahm.com, you'll find that we're offering free group-study guides in both six- and twelve- week lengths. Why not gather a group of work-at-home moms and *Do Life Different* together?

In all things, let His Words carry you through.

Cease striving and know that I am God.
Psalm 46:10

Do Life Different

"Whatever you do, work at it with all your heart, as working for the Lord ..."

Colossians 3:23a

1. no more excuses

> *The words of Amos, one of the shepherds of Tekoa.*
> *Amos 1:1a NIV*

Do you ever wonder if your life is of use to God? Can God really use you to make a difference in the world?

I recently found a little nugget about this as I was reading in the Old Testament. Amos 1:1 (NIV) says, "The words of Amos, one of the shepherds of Tekoa – the vision he saw concerning Israel two years before the earthquake, when Uzziah was king of Judah and Jeroboam son of Jehoash, was king of Israel."

Amos was a prophet in Israel, and a book of the Bible is named after him. Before Amos' call by God as a prophet, he was a simple shepherd. God chose a nobody, plucked him out from among the sheep, and asked him to speak to the nation of Israel—to speak the very words of God: His warnings and calls to repentance. God used a shepherd. Incredible. He could have used a king or a rich and powerful man, but instead He chose a shepherd.

Jill Hart

When I meet women and ask them what they do, I get a lot of different responses. The answers that especially catch my attention are those that start with I'm just...

"I'm just a stay-at-home mom."
"Oh, I'm just a sales rep."
"I'm just a writer."

I used to do the same thing. But over the years, I've come to realize that saying we're *just* anything robs God of His glory. He places us where we are for a reason. He *chose* me to live out the calling He's given me. He *chose* you to make a difference right where you are. As a mom, a business owner — whatever job He's called you to.

Next time you think, God could never use me, or I'm just _ (fill in the blank) _, catch yourself.

I truly believe God loves a challenge, and He uses those of us who seem insignificant, or not good enough, or like we just don't have it all together.

We're the ones He uses.

Next time you find yourself responding to the question of what you do with *I'm just* — stop. And remember, you are a woman called by God to be a light in this world.

Video devo 1 is available at www.dolifedifferent.org

Do Life Different

Doing it different: Do you find yourself doubting God can use you? Ask Him to show you new ways to step out in confidence.

2. a woman of noble character

A wife of noble character who can find? She is worth far more than rubies. Proverbs 31:10 NIV

In college I first came across the Proverbs 31 woman. I'd heard the passage before in church, but hadn't really paid attention to the woman this chapter introduces. In fact, when I read it, verse ten tripped me up. *A wife of noble character.* What does that mean?

The word "noble" always seemed like a snobby word to me. I can't remember when I've ever been called noble. It sounds like something you would use to describe the Queen of England, not a housewife. However, according to dictionary definitions, noble means to possess outstanding qualities, to have good character, and to be a decent person at heart.

There are several women in my life that come to mind when I think of people who possess outstanding qualities. In fact, my mom would be at the top of my list.

Do Life Different

Who comes to mind when you think of women who possess outstanding qualities? Who is a living, breathing example of the fruits of the Spirit: love, joy, peace, forbearance, kindness, goodness, faithfulness, gentleness, and self-control? These are women you're drawn to. Who do you look forward to spending time with? Women who speak truth into your life ... even when you don't want to hear it.

So, how do *we* go about becoming noble women?

First and foremost, we must believe in Jesus and turn our lives over to Him. When we accept God's gift of salvation, we are then filled with the Holy Spirit. And only the Holy Spirit can produce the list of qualities we just discussed.

We also need to spend time regularly in God's Word. Not as something to check off our to-do list, but to see how God wants us to live, to learn about His grace, and to be changed by Him. God's Word is living and active. He changes us from the inside out.

Even if you read and meditate on one verse a day, it will make all the difference. When my kids were small and quiet alone time didn't exist, I'd make it my goal to read one verse out of the book of Proverbs every day.

Jill Hart

In our pursuit to become women who possess outstanding qualities, women who radiate God's joy, we must surround ourselves with other women of noble character. Choose your closest friends from women with a contagious dose of God's joy.

Video devo 2 is available at www.dolifedifferent.org

Doing it different: Are there friendships you could cultivate that would draw you closer to God? Reach out to someone who will call you to a higher place of nobility.

_____

_____

_____

_____

_____

_____

_____

_____

3. full confidence

Her husband has full confidence in her.
Proverbs 31:11a NIV

As I read this verse recently, the words "full confidence" jumped out at me. What does it really mean to have full confidence in someone? As we look at the example of the Proverbs 31 woman, we can see she managed both her household and her business. She sold cloth, bought fields, and planted vineyards. Her husband trusted her with those decisions.

This doesn't look that different for work-at-home moms in the 21st century. If we're running home-based businesses and raising our kids at the same time, our spouse has to be able to trust we'll handle both well. We have to balance getting our work done, managing the finances of the business (and possibly our household finances as well) and spending time with our children, caring for, and disciplining them.

Thankfully, we can place our full confidence in our Heavenly Father. We can depend on Him when we're feeling overwhelmed or frustrated.

We'll let our husbands down from time to time. We'll make mistakes. And our spouses will let us down as well. But God will never let us down. He is faithful through and through.

As I look back over the years of my marriage, I can see where I made so many mistakes, yet God walked through them with me. My husband and I were careless with our credit card spending when first married. We had to learn the hard way how to buckle down and pay off that debt. Even though it's completely our fault we had debt to deal with, God has repeatedly been merciful to us, allowing us to settle some of it for pennies on the dollar.

We can carry this same attitude of graciousness into our marriages. We can choose to be wives who forgive as we've been forgiven. We can choose to be wise women who depend on God and in whom our husbands can have *full confidence.*

Video devo 3 is available at www.dolifedifferent.org

Do Life Different

Doing it different: Do you feel your husband has full confidence in you? What areas of your life might need to change in order to get closer to this goal?

_____
_____
_____
_____
_____
_____
_____
_____
_____
_____
_____
_____
_____
_____
_____

4. eager

> *She selects wool and flax and works with eager hands.*
> *Proverbs 31:13 NIV*

What about your business, or work-at-home job, do you love? Is there a certain aspect of your work that excites you each morning?

As we see in today's verse, the woman in Proverbs 31 worked with "eager hands." We're also told in the Proverbs 31 passage she woke early (v 15) and then burned the midnight oil (v 18). Many of us know what that feels like. It seems there are never enough hours in the day to get everything done. Yet, when we're doing something we love, something we're passionate about, we can work with eager hands well into the night hours.

The work you love to do, the tasks that come easily and give a sense of fulfillment reveal your true passion. Take a moment to think about what types of things you love to do. If you love working with children, maybe running a daycare would be right for you. If you love sewing, maybe you could offer that service to others. If you love to write, maybe it's time to pursue that dream.

Expert Marcus Buckingham gave a talk on how to find our passion in business. His talk centered on knowing our strengths as well as our weaknesses. He quoted a study his company had done, asking thousands of women whether they should focus on fixing weaknesses or building up their strengths to become better business owners. 70% said they tended to focus on fixing weaknesses.

Buckingham pointed out when we focus on fixing our perceived weaknesses, and ignore our strengths we fight against our God-given talent. It's when we learn to live in our strengths and develop them we find success. We don't want to ignore our weaknesses, but we want to focus our main energies on finding and building the strengths God placed within us.

This played out in my business life. I figured out numbers, and accounting, are not where my strengths reside. I tried to handle my own bookkeeping when I started my business. As my business grew, so did the mess I was making out of my books. I (finally) hired an accountant who not only handles my taxes, but the bookkeeping as well. What a relief!

Jill Hart

Now I spend time doing what I do well instead of beating myself up trying to handle tasks in my weak areas.

Take a look at how you run your business. Where do you see your strengths shining through? How can you restructure so you build up those strengths and use them each day?

Video devo 4 is available at www.dolifedifferent.org

Doing it different: How can you plan things so you wake with eager hands, excited to get each day started?

_____

_____

_____

_____

_____

_____

_____

_____

_____

5. the joy of the morning

She gets up while it is still night; she provides food for her family and portions for her female servants.
Proverbs 31:15 NIV

When I first read Proverbs 31, verse 15, I nearly closed my Bible. I've never been a morning person. I especially hated mornings during college years. To think the model woman woke before dark...and not only that, but she woke to cook? Ugh.

For several years, this verse was a stumbling block for me. I felt I'd never attain (honestly, I'd never *want* to attain) the attitude of servanthood the Proverbs 31 woman embodies. I couldn't imagine wanting to wake up early to work or care for a family. I was doomed to failure.

I laugh as I'm writing this at six o'clock in the morning. I'm still not a morning person. I'll probably need a nap later, but it's amazing what becoming a mother has done to me. I want the best for my kids, and I want to spend time with them. So, if that means working in the early morning hours or late at night, so I can spend my days with them, it's well worth it.

There are many characteristics of the Proverbs 31 woman that can feel overwhelming when we read them as a whole. But when we look at her actions verse by verse, we can sense that her love for her family and her love for God are what drive her. And what we are to exemplify.

Even if I never woke at six o'clock to work, I'd find other ways to make sure my family came first. We must be careful not to compare ourselves to the Proverbs 31 woman or any other woman. God has created us to be just who we are. Different sizes, different shapes, and different styles.

When we set aside comparisons—what we think we must act like to be a good mom or a good wife or a good business owner—we can step into the person God created us to be. If there are things we need to change, we can make those changes because they better us, not because we're trying to keep up with or outdo someone else.

Video devo 5 is available at www.dolifedifferent.org

Do Life Different

Doing it different: Are there areas in your life where you're trying to keep up with others? What do you need to let go in order to find peace?

_____
_____
_____
_____
_____
_____
_____
_____
_____
_____
_____
_____
_____
_____
_____
_____
_____
_____
_____

6. making wise decisions

She sees that her trading is profitable, and her lamp does not go out at night. Proverbs 31:18 NIV

This verse is one of my favorites because it points out an aspect of the Proverbs 31 woman I truly admire: her wisdom. Parts of this chapter tell us about this woman's businesses (she makes and sells linen cloths, she sells fields, and buys and plants vineyards) and the above verse is no exception. It's great business advice.

It shows us, not only does she manage business; she takes the time to look over her accounts. She keeps watch on what succeeds and works to promote that. I tend to avoid looking at the financial statements for my business. It can be overwhelming (and often discouraging) to see where things stand. But, it does motivate me to continue building my business.

This woman is not afraid of facing the truth. She's not afraid to evaluate her work and make changes to keep her business profitable.

I'm a jump-and-then-look type of girl. My husband is much more logical. He's the one who keeps me grounded and asks me to stop, look things over, and think through decisions. I'm constantly coming up with new brilliant ideas and he consistently reminds me to plan the details before moving forward. Details are not where the fun lies for me.

However, over the years I've come to understand how important the details truly are. I've run with an idea that wasn't fully formed and landed flat on my face.

The Proverbs 31 woman clearly sees that to care for her family well, to make the time she spends on her business worthwhile, she must be a good steward of it. Being excited about an idea or a business is great, but it will only carry you so far.

The key to long-term success is to follow the example of this woman and keep a close eye on your business. What's working? What isn't working? What changes will help your business be profitable?

Our focus should not be solely on making money, but we do need to be wise in how we run our business so it benefits our family, not drains it. We must nurture, discipline, and care for our businesses like we do our families. Just as we need to be proactive and intentional with how we raise our children, we must also be so with the businesses God blessed us with.

Video devo 6 is available at www.dolifedifferent.org

Doing it different: What areas of your business need an honest evaluation? How can you address necessary changes in a swift and wise manner?

7. God's economy

She opens her arms to the poor and extends her hands to the needy. Proverbs 31:20 NIV

Proverbs 31:20 is a beautiful reminder of how God asks us to live each day of our lives. We are called to simply love God and love others. (Deuteronomy 6:5) If we do these two things, we fulfill God's primary mission for us.

When we're in business it's easy to forget that mission. To think our time here on Earth is to be spent seeking success, that our end-goal is financial.

It's easy to get mixed up, because God's economy is upside down. To lead, we must serve (Matthew 20:26). To get, we must give (Deuteronomy 15:10).

The world tells us success is found by making money or being known. That what we're doing doesn't really matter unless we're getting some kind of payoff out of it. True success, godly success, means being obedient, using our businesses as a ministry to help others.

We sometimes think God doesn't care about our success. Maybe He's busy with other things or our financial reality is beyond His reach. I would argue God does care about our success, but His definition of success is very different from ours.

He wants more for us than we want for ourselves. He also knows what we need.

I was walking in a clothing store not long ago and saw a pretty older woman looking at clothing near the clearance rack where I had stationed myself. I stayed there for a moment, watching her out of the corner of my eye.

I could only afford clothing on the clearance rack of this particular store. She could have had anything in the store. But what caught my eye was how sad she looked. Maybe she just had a bad day. Maybe she was sad about being alone. I'll never know.

I walked away from the store that day realizing though my funds may be limited, I'm abundantly blessed in other areas: family, friends, the CWAHM (Christian Work at Home Mom) community…my faith in God. I wouldn't trade those relationships for all the money in the world, even if it meant I could buy two

Do Life Different

of everything in that store. I was filled with peace and joy at the thought.

It boils down to thankfulness. We can live a life of gratitude by being generous with however much God has given us. Give to your local church. Give to local business owners. Give to those we see in need. Whether your business makes lots of money or just a little, give, as you're able.

Video devo 7 is available at www.dolifedifferent.org

Doing it different: How can you express your gratitude to God in a new way? How can you use that expression of gratitude to influence others?

_____

_____

_____

_____

_____

_____

_____

8. overcoming fear and worry

She is clothed with strength and dignity; she can laugh at the days to come. Proverbs 31:25 NIV

Have you ever known anyone who "laughed at the days to come?" What type of person would be able to do that? In my mind, someone who can laugh at the days to come would be someone full of confidence in her God. Someone full of peace.

When I read this verse, God speaks to my heart, reminding me we can be at peace even in this chaotic world.

Several dictionaries define peace as being free from fear. Isn't that a beautiful thought? Can you imagine living free from all fear? Is it actually possible to set aside worry about the future and of the unknown?

Not long after I began pondering God's peace, I found a familiar passage in Galatians 5 that tells us about the fruit of the Spirit. One of them jumped out at me: peace!

Do Life Different

Peace is spiritual gift. A peaceful life is developed as we mature in Christ. As we get to know Him better, and walk more closely with Him, peace is gifted to us by the Spirit and only attainable through the Spirit's power.

This will sound a bit silly, but I carry around a little book of promises by Max Lucado in my purse. *Fear Not* is full of Lucado quotes and tons of Scripture. Every time I start getting that panicky feeling in my stomach, or another symptom of fear and worry, I pull it out. I read until the Holy Spirit takes away the fear. I soak in those glorious passages until I'm full of His peace that chases away all worry.

The more I do this, the more I'm able to combat negative thought patterns with God's words. I've read some of the passages so many times I can quote them when I start to worry. God's truth has lodged itself in my heart and helps me to stand firm against fear, worry, and doubt.

There are many things we have no control over or that we can do anything about. When we turn every burden over to Christ, we know even the too-big things are in His hands.

And He does want to hear all of our worries and fears. He is our refuge, our hiding place, our safety.

Jill Hart

"Trust in him at all times, you people; pour out your hearts to him, for God is our refuge." Psalm 62:8 (NIV)

Video devo 8 is available at www.dolifedifferent.org

Doing it different: What is a new way you can chase the doubt and fear away whenever they creep in?

_____
_____
_____
_____
_____
_____
_____
_____
_____
_____
_____

9. seeking wisdom

She speaks with wisdom, and faithful instruction is on her tongue. Proverbs 31:26 NIV

We wear a lot of different hats. Wife, mom, business owner, friend. Sometimes it's more than we can handle, too many roles require decision-making and wisdom. Wisdom feels is in short supply, yet it's what we need the most.

A wise woman uses discernment, insight, and good sense.

Oh, how I long to be a woman of wisdom! Someone who makes astute decisions. Someone with insight and discernment into others needs. However, I often feel like a fawn learning to walk when it comes to wisdom. I think I know what these legs of mine are supposed to do, but I keep getting tangled up and fall on my face. I think I know what wisdom should look like, so I jump forward into what makes sense to me. And then—splat! Right on my face again.

The problem we tend to have with godly wisdom is that God's ways often don't make sense in this world, especially when it comes to business. The world tells us to out look for ourselves and take what we can get at every turn. God tells us to care for one another, to treat each other with love.

We try to follow worldly business advice and then we're frustrated when it doesn't work the way it seems to work for others. I can't tell you how many times I've purchased a business book by a respected expert in the corporate world. I follow their advice, but somehow it doesn't turn out the way I expect.

And then there are the times I manage to lay my business at Jesus' feet. I hand it all to Jesus and ask Him to do with it what He desires, to lead me as I walk forward. And He does. When I submit my head, my heart, and my business to the Lord – these are often when unexpected opportunities arise.

Opportunities I couldn't have created for myself.

Video devo 9 is available at www.dolifedifferent.org

Do Life Different

Doing it different: Have you given your business over to God? What portions of your business do you need to lay at His feet today?

_____
_____
_____
_____
_____
_____
_____
_____
_____
_____
_____
_____
_____
_____
_____
_____
_____
_____

10. striving to please God

Charm is deceptive, and beauty is fleeting; but a woman who fears the LORD is to be praised. Proverbs 31:30 NIV

We often think of this verse in terms of how we should live our daily lives, but today let's think of it in terms of how we might live as business owners.

Our businesses can be filled with prayer. We can seek Him on a personal level, but also in business.

I keep a list of prayer requests updated regularly. There are several pages for friends and family, but I also keep pages about my business. That my website would bless the visitors. That God would provide for my team and meet the needs only He knows. That God would grow CWAHM to become what He desires.

I also pray God will keep me flexible with my schedule and open to His leading. I've found starting each day open to not only what's on my to-do list, but what God brings my way lightens stress

Do Life Different

and offers many wonderful opportunities I'd have missed otherwise.

We can choose an open attitude, asking how to minister to others, instead of focusing solely on our businesses and ourselves.

When I began working from home my schedule was more rigid. As my kids have grown, the schedule has had to relax a little. As I mature spiritually, I've found there are days when God brings a person or a need to mind that might keep me from working at all.

It was hard to put down my plans for the day in favor of what God had in store. But, I'm learning that His plans are always better and my business can survive if I don't finish my to-do list every single day.

It is easy to forget that our businesses are ministries. There's a fine line between being effective for the Kingdom and being a good steward of your finances, resources, and plans. Though it's always important to engage good business practices, we can miss opportunities to be the hands and feet of Jesus if we get too attached to our lists and planners. Instead, let's live in our careers as godly women like the example of the Proverbs 31 woman sets.

Video devo 10 is available at www.dolifedifferent.org

Jill Hart

Doing it different: How can you integrate prayer into your business life in new ways this week?

11. pursuing excellence when we feel mediocre

> But Moses said to God, "Who am I that I should go to Pharaoh and bring the Israelites out of Egypt?"
> Exodus 3:11 NIV

More days than not, I roll out of bed expecting the ordinary. Sure, there are times when I know something exciting is on the calendar. Most days, however, are pretty similar: get out of bed, exercise, spend time with the kids, work, feed the family, watch TV, go to bed. Sprinkle in laundry and housework throughout, and that pretty much sums up my life.

In this passage, we find Moses stuck in a rut, too. He expected to get up, watch his father-in-law's sheep, and then head home. Typical day.

Instead, Moses notices a bush on fire but not burning up. Then he hears the voice of Almighty God speaking from the bush.

So what does he do? He proceeds to argue with God, insisting that God had the wrong guy.

I'm pretty sure if I heard God talking to me from a burning bush, I wouldn't have the guts to question Him, let alone to argue. But Moses seems to have no problem calling God out on His mistake.

"Who am I that I should go to Pharaoh and bring the Israelites out of Egypt?"

What I love best about this passage, though, is what comes next. Moses tells God several times that he isn't the man for the job. Every time God answers with words like, "*I will be with you*" and "*I will help you.*" He doesn't say, "*Moses you're a great guy. You can do it.*"

No. God reminds Moses of whom HE is.

God is the one who does the miracles in this story and every other story in Scripture. Never do we see God leaving us to rely on our own strength. When He calls us to do something, God believes in us because He will be with us, guiding us, and working behind the scenes.

When we're called by God to do something great, we can walk forward in confidence trusting that He has the right person. No matter how mediocre we feel. We choose obedience; God does the rest.

Do Life Different

Video devo 11 is available at www.dolifedifferent.org

Doing it different: What is God calling you to do that requires you to step outside your comfort zone? Can you put your faith in Him and go for it?

_____
_____
_____
_____
_____
_____
_____
_____
_____
_____
_____
_____
_____

12. the balancing act

But seek first his kingdom and his righteousness, and all these things will be given to you as well. Matthew 6:33 NIV

When I do interviews about working from home, I get asked one question more than any other: *How do you balance it all?* My answer never changes. Balance, to some degree, is a myth. Life for work-at-home moms is a constant juggling act: an ongoing play with acts, characters, and ever-changing scenes. As our kids grow, their needs change. As our businesses grow, those needs change as well. There is no secret formula to balancing it all perfectly.

I am constantly re-evaluating to see where things stand in each area of my life and to make changes as necessary.

Despite all the juggling, working from home is worth every ounce of effort.

On days when the balance feels off or seems like I'm going to drop one of the many balls in the air, I've had to learn to relax. Sometimes those balls will fall. Sometimes we need to set a ball down. If you're feeling the stress of balancing, take a deep breath, take a step back, and give yourself a break. We all struggle. We all need to take inventory and make adjustments in our schedules on a regular basis.

The one thing that keeps me grounded in the midst of the busyness is focusing on God above all else. When I'm focused on myself, what I can accomplish, or bringing in an income, I flounder. I get desperate. I make stupid decisions. When I focus on God, my perspective shifts and I'm able to see people and events through the lens of His love.

When we seek Him first, the rest falls into place.

That brings us to the next part of the verse, "… all these things will be given to you as well." Does it mean if we live focused on God, He will give us lots of good things? Not necessarily.

The preceding verses talk about clothing and food. For most of us, these may not generally be our primary concerns. Most of us have the food, shelter, and clothing we need. However, we seem to constantly want *more*.

I believe we need to focus on the Lord and ask Him to give us eyes that see all the good things He has already provided. Instead of expecting more, we can live grateful for the abundance we already enjoy.

Video devo 12 is available at www.dolifedifferent.org

Doing it different: What expectations or priorities keep you striving for more? If you balance those, what can you naturally eliminate from your schedule?

13. business as ministry

Take delight in the LORD, and he will give you the desires of your heart. Psalm 37:4 NIV

How do we mesh business and ministry in a way that stays true to our missions and our needs?

I can't tell you how many times I've asked myself this question. It's seems like the two should co-exist. Yet we're taught that the end-goal in business is financial gain. The end-goal in ministry is life change. So, how do we put them together without creating tension by trying to do both?

I recently took this question to my pastor. He responded by telling me something that made so much sense. Something I *knew* somewhere deep inside, but really needed the reminder.

He said, "It's a heart thing."

If your heart is set on making money at all costs, then your life and your business will look exactly that way. You won't have room for pro-bono work or time to chat with someone who needs a listening ear.

If your heart is set on helping others in your own power then your life will reflect that. You'll fall prey to every bleeding heart and probably never make a dime.

The answer lies somewhere in between. Setting our hearts on God, delighting in Him, and letting Him direct our business steps. When we let the Spirit of God guide us, we'll feel His nudge to forgive a debt or give something at a reduced cost. And we'll be confident in charging regular customers, trusting God will provide for them financially as He does for us.

It's all about where our heart is.

Yes, God will give us the desires of our hearts, but there's a double meaning. God gives us our desires, and He created us, so He planted our desires, our calling within us.

If He called us to work from home or run a business, who better to guide us through every step?

Video devo 13 is available at www.dolifedifferent.org

Doing it different: Where is your heart on the financial-gain/life-change continuum? Ask God to show you if you're out of balance and how to make it right.

_____
_____
_____
_____
_____
_____
_____
_____
_____
_____
_____
_____
_____
_____
_____
_____
_____
_____

14. taking steps of faith

It is for freedom that Christ has set us free. Stand firm, then, and do not let yourselves be burdened again by a yoke of slavery. Galatians 5:1 NIV

God did miraculous things to get the Israelites out of Egypt. He sent Moses and Aaron to deliver them. He sent locusts, frogs, and other plagues to change the heart of Pharaoh. He parted the sea so the Israelites could walk through on dry land. And then He brought that same sea back together to drown the Egyptian army chasing them.

God did all this, yet when they get to the Promised Land, the Israelites still aren't sure God can do what He says He will do. So, when the time comes for them to cross over into the Promised Land, they send spies ahead. You know, just to check and be *sure* it's safe for them to enter the land God has promised them.

Twelve spies go and scout things out. When they come back, ten say, "No way. We can't do this." They point out seemingly insurmountable obstacles like giants and other nations already dwelling there. Only two say, "Yes, we should go." Only two trust God to see them through. They admit the ten are right; that it will be hard to conquer the other nations, but they believe God can bring them victory.

Despite the urging of the two, the Israelites decide they aren't ready to trust God to give them this land. They grumble Moses (and God) brought them out of Egypt to die or worse yet, to be the slaves of other nations.

And so God tells them to turn around. To go back into the desert. (Deut 1:40)

They were literally across the river from the Promised Land. They were *so* close. Now they'll spend another forty years wandering in the desert. The Israelites are kept out of their physical promised land by their doubt, grumbling, and conceit.

We're promised freedom when we come to know Christ. Freedom is our promised land as Christians. Christ delivered us from the laws that burdened the nation of Israel for thousands of years. Yet many of us still try to earn our salvation, believing there's something we must do to make ourselves worthy of the love of God.

Jill Hart

We wander in the desert of loneliness and despair, trying to find our way to God on our own. But the only way to God is through Christ.

Video devo 14 is available at www.dolifedifferent.org

Doing it different: Reject the instinct to work for God's favor. How can you walk in His grace and freedom in new ways this week?

15. starting fresh

Because of the LORD's great love we are not consumed, for his compassions never fail. They are new every morning; great is your faithfulness. Lamentations 3:22-23 NIV

I love to read stories of underdogs who, despite mistakes, triumph in the end. I think most of us love stories of redemption. Second chances. Starting over.

And we hope for that same redemption in our own lives as well.

Maybe yesterday wasn't great. Maybe last week was awful. Maybe this entire year has been one hot mess after another. Trust me, I know that feeling. Just recently I spent the day apologizing and cleaning up the destruction I'd caused in a relationship.

But, there is beauty amidst the ashes, a silver lining in every storm cloud. God's Word confirms we can start over with Him every morning. He knows we are human and that we'll need chance after chance to get things right.

Thankfully, as the verse above reminds us, God's mercies are new every morning.

A fresh start *every* morning. What a great thought.

If we rose with each new day and faced it with that attitude, imagine what our lives would be like. What if you stood from your bed tomorrow and said, "This is going to be a *great* day. God's mercies are new, and I can start over fresh with Him today." At worst, it'd put a smile on your face that you talk to yourself. At best, you'd start out with an entirely new perspective.

We can breathe deeply each morning because we have a clean slate with God. It also allows us to extend that grace to those around us. The customer who sent the mean email yesterday? Let it go. The frustration you felt when putting your kids to bed last night? Let it go. The anger you're harboring toward yourself for that mistake? Yep, time to let that go as well.

Today is a new day!

I often write verses on 3" x 5" cards and put them on our bathroom mirror. It's one of my favorite tactics to let what God is teaching sink in.

Video devo 15 is available at www.dolifedifferent.org

Do Life Different

Doing it different: What new tactic can you employ to remind yourself to delight in God's renewed mercies each day?

_____
_____
_____
_____
_____
_____
_____
_____
_____
_____
_____
_____
_____

16. don't hide from your calling

> *So they inquired further of the Lord, "Has the man come here yet?" And the Lord said, "Yes. He has hidden himself among the supplies."* 1 Samuel 10:22 NIV

As we step into this story, Saul has just been chosen as the first king of Israel. Chosen by God Almighty and anointed by the prophet Samuel.

Not long after Samuel tells Saul that he will be King, Samuel calls all the tribes of Israel together to make it official. He passes through each family until he comes to Saul's family. He calls out for Saul, son of Kish. But Saul is nowhere to be found.

In fact, they have to ask the Lord about Saul's whereabouts before they can locate him. Come to find out, he is hiding behind the baggage. He is terrified of this new calling of God on his life.

I can so relate.

Do Life Different

We often hide behind our own baggage, don't we? We let the self-doubt seep in and we douse ourselves with our own unkind words. I often catch myself in negative self-talk. *No one wants to listen to you. You're no one special.*

I hide behind the baggage of my past. Partly because I know some of those things I say to myself have a grain of truth to them. (I really am pretty boring most of the time.) Partly because I let my baggage shape who I am today. And partly because I am afraid of stepping up and doing what God has called me to do.

So, I hide behind the baggage, speaking cruel words to myself. And then I wonder why I don't feel fulfilled and happy.

It's time to make a change. It's time to step out from behind the baggage and into the truth of who God says we are, who we can be with His help.

Do you fill your head with mean-girl thoughts about yourself, too? Are you hiding behind the fear and baggage like Saul?

Video devo 16 is available at www.dolifedifferent.org

Doing it different: Mentally pack a suitcase with your insecurities and self-doubt. Turn your back on your baggage and leave it in the past. How can you live in front of your baggage this week?

17. i'll handle this

> Because you relied on the king of Aram and not on the LORD your God, the army of the king of Aram has escaped from your hand. 2 Chronicles 16:7b NIV

King Asa was one of the many kings who ruled over Judah. There were Kings who obeyed God and many more who chose not to. King Asa was one who followed God ... mostly.

During Asa's reign, Israel and Judah were separate countries. At one point, Israel decided to attack King Asa and Judah. Instead of seeking God's wisdom when Israel attacked, King Asa chose to handle it on his own. The king had spent years reforming Israel and removing idols from the land, but now he thinks he can make a treaty with Aram and handle the mess alone.

Isn't that how our minds work, too? Oh, I can get this one, God! I won't need your help with this mess. Aren't you proud of me for handling it myself, Lord?

But, the truth is, God isn't proud of us when we walk forward without consulting Him. Because King Asa tried to handle the mess on his own, he ended up in an even *bigger* mess. I've certainly seen this scenario play out in my own life.

I can name several ideas I've had that I thought would be great projects for CWAHM. Some I patiently talked through with my husband and prayed about, only moving forward when I felt confident I had the green light. But others I jumped into without talking to anyone. Because I think they'll say no. So I don't ask. I just plow ahead and end up in a mess of my own making.

The passage in 2 Chronicles recounts the times that Asa had experienced victory over other nations because He sought God first. But this time he didn't. So he failed.

This is one lesson from the past I hope we'll take to heart. Seek God first. Avoid the mess.

Video devo 17 is available at www.dolifedifferent.org

Do Life Different

Doing it different: When have you "handled things" rather than asking God for wisdom and direction? What changes can help you remember to put God first – even when you think things are under control?

_____
_____
_____
_____
_____
_____
_____
_____
_____
_____
_____
_____
_____
_____
_____
_____
_____

Jill Hart

18. fulfill your calling

> *In everything that he undertook in the service of God's temple and in obedience to the law and the commands, he sought his God and worked wholeheartedly. And so he prospered.* 2 Chronicles 31:21 NIV

You may have heard of King Hezekiah. His story is pretty amazing. He becomes king at age twenty-five and immediately sets out to restore the land and tear down the idols the Israelites had been worshipping.

Hezekiah restores the land to godliness. He restores the priests and asks them to cleanse and purify the temple. He reinstates Passover.

More than that, Hezekiah goes to the temple and bows down before God. A king bowing before the King of Kings. Isn't that a powerful picture?

King Hezekiah is a beautiful example for us work-at-home moms. He gave himself fully to his work for God. His calling—being King—was his work for God.

He did it to the best of his ability, seeking God at every turn.

Sometimes we feel as if our calling is inadequate. I longed for many years to be a missionary, thinking of that as the highest calling God could put on a woman's life.

But, during my years as a mom and a business owner, I've begun to understand that God almost always calls us to minister in our closest sphere of influence before taking us to the next level. He wants us to impact our families, our churches, and local communities. He wanted King Hezekiah to clean up his own life. Only then could Hezekiah be the example for his kingdom.

No matter what God calls us to do, we can do it to the best of our ability – for God. When I'm intentional with my kids, when I make wise business decisions, when I put another's needs before my own, I'm serving God. We need to show our faithfulness in the things that seem small. We need to minister in the areas of our lives where there may not be fanfare or recognition, just as we do in the bigger areas God may call us to.

Jill Hart

What's your calling? Do you struggle with the misconception only missionaries and pastors work for God?

Video devo 18 is available at www.dolifedifferent.org

Doing it different: How can you be like Hezekiah and live in surrendered abandon this week?

19. do the work

> *David also said to Solomon his son, "Be strong and courageous, and do the work. Do not be afraid or discouraged, for the Lord God, my God, is with you. He will not fail you or forsake you until all the work for the service of the temple of the Lord is finished. 1 Chronicles 28:20 NIV*

Elderly King David passes his kingdom over to his son, Solomon. David dreamed for many years of building a temple to the Lord. God, however, has told David that his son, Solomon, will be the one to build His temple.

David spent many years amassing all of the tools and supplies Solomon would need to build the most magnificent temple possible. He knows God will be with his son as he begins work. However, he also knows Solomon has to choose to do this in obedience to God.

David wants Solomon to be *strong and brave and do the work*. David has lived a full life and knew what both obedience and disobedience brought about in a person's life. He knows that doing the work of God's calling is an act of the will. It's to do whatever God has asked, and then stepping forward with His help to act.

Solomon can choose to do God's work ... or choose not to.

This same principle holds true in our lives today. We can be strong and brave and live out our life calling. We can fight through the fear and fight what our adversary throws at us.

Or we can let fear and selfishness take over and say no to God's calling. We can foolishly follow our own paths and desires, ignoring the work God has laid before us.

There have been many such choices in my life. When I wrote my first book, I was crippled by fear. I knew deep down it was the next step God asked me to take, but I was terrified of failing. Oh how happy I am that I allowed God to walk me through that journey.

Video devo 19 is available at www.dolifedifferent.org

Do Life Different

Doing it different: What choices are you facing that you're afraid to say yes to? Is there an area in which you need to buckle down and do the work?

20. it's a choice

All Judah rejoiced about the oath because they had sworn it wholeheartedly. They sought God eagerly, and he was found by them. So the Lord gave them rest on every side.
2 Chronicles 15:15 NIV

Our human nature leans toward disobedience. We want to do our own thing. I'd often rather snuggle up by a fire with a book and a cup of hot cocoa than sit at my desk and work. I'd definitely rather nap than exercise.

It's an act of the will to be obedient and do what needs to be done.

Obedience is hard. It usually involves setting our desires and natural tendencies aside. That's not something most of us do easily.

In the passage above, the people of Israel were happy about King Asa's promise to obey God. They followed his example and the entire country recommitted to God. What an amazing thought. Can you imagine what our country would look like if our leaders recommitted to God ... and then the entire country followed suit?

The same can be true on a smaller scale in our homes. Several years ago my husband was caught up in a computer game. He played several hours a day after work and many evenings our kids, who were very small at the time, would go to bed without really getting quality time with him. Maybe a few minutes at the dinner table, if that.

Eventually it affected our marriage, his relationships with the kids, and even his performance at work. It was discouraging, and despite my fervent prayers, I wasn't sure things would ever change.

God, however, had other plans. Through a series of events, God softened my husband's heart and opened his eyes. My husband put down his computer mouse one night and said he was done. I didn't fully believe it at the time, but it's been five years now, and I can testify he recommitted his life to God and has never returned to gaming.

My husband's recommitment to God changed all of our lives. Our family followed his example and our hearts were changed, too.

Look for God. You will find Him. Or better yet, He will find you. If you're looking to make a change, looking to live a life of obedience, seek Him wholeheartedly.

He is the God of second chances.

Video devo 20 is available at www.dolifedifferent.org

Doing it different: What important disciplines are difficult for you? Pick one or two and make a commitment to follow through with God's help.

21. your response counts

Then David said to Nathan, "I have sinned against the LORD." 2 Samuel 12:13 NIV

I love to read the stories of the kings in the Old Testament. It's inspiring to see how God works in their lives and what they accomplish when obedient to God's commands. Some of the kings were incredibly good, God-following leaders. Others were disobedient and generally ended up leading the nation of Israel into dark times of oppression and idol worship.

I read some of these "king stories" not long ago and realized something else sets them apart from one another ... their responses to God's discipline.

Take, for example, King Uzziah (2 Chron 26). He takes it upon himself to go into the temple of the Lord and burn incense, a job only priests to do. The priests tell the king what he's done was not right. At this point, King Uzziah has two choices: he can own up to his sinful actions and repent, or he can deny any wrongdoing and rage against God and his accusers.

Unfortunately, Uzziah takes the path of destruction. He rages against the priests for daring to question his actions. He takes no responsibility for his actions and instead tries to places blame anywhere but on himself. Then while still in the middle of his temper tantrum, leprosy broke out on his forehead. He was never healed and "… lived in a separate house—leprous, and banned from the temple of the Lord." His son took charge of the kingdom.

Now let's look at the life of King David for a moment. We know David sinned with Bathsheba. However, when the prophet Nathan called him out on what he'd done, David didn't try to push the blame on someone else. He didn't scream and rage and throw a fit. David took responsibility for his actions. He repented.

There were still consequences for David's sin, but he was able to make right his relationship with the Lord. David went on to rule for many more years eventually passing his kingdom on to Bathsheba's son Solomon.

What do *our* lives look like when God brings sin to our attention? Do we act like King Uzziah and throw a fit, determined not to accept the responsibility? Or do we take the path David chose and bow in humble repentance before God?

Video devo 21 is available at www.dolifedifferent.org

Doing it different: Is there something in your life God has been asking you to repent of? It's time to acknowledge it, repent, and move on in a restored relationship with Christ.

_____
_____
_____
_____
_____
_____
_____
_____
_____
_____
_____
_____

22. serving God not people

Then Saul said to Samuel, "I have sinned. I violated the Lord's command and your instructions. I was afraid of the men and so I gave in to them. 1 Samuel 15:24 NIV

Being in business can be hard. There is so much advice available, much of it from successful business people telling you to "look out for number one." We all want to be successful. It's easy to feel like you need to give into the pressure to do things the world's way. While worldly business principles are not necessarily sinful, the attitudes behind them can be if we put our worldly success ahead of kingdom purpose.

When Saul was made King, he fell into the trap of listening to the people who told him to do contrary to what God said. Saul was afraid of losing the respect of these people and did what they said instead of holding steady and being obedient to God.

I've listened to many seminars over the years on many different business topics. I went to one such webinar the other day. It was full of solid marketing information, but when I hung up the phone afterward I couldn't shake the feeling that I wasn't supposed to follow this person's advice.

As I thought through it some more, I realized that while the advice given made sense for a business that was only worried about making a profit, it didn't make sense for my ministry. God challenged me to once again go against the flow and trust Him to provide by running my business His way.

God's economy is upside down. To get, we must give. To find joy, we must serve. To be content with ourselves, we must put others' needs before our own. It makes no sense that these business practices would work, but God's mysterious ways keep astounding me day after day by bringing new customers and opportunities my way.

When forming a plan of action for our businesses, we must be careful not to simply copy everyone else. We need to be God-focused even in our business systems. It's imperative we know whom in our lives we can trust, not just to tell us what we want to hear, but to tell us what God says.

Before making business decisions, let's seek godly counsel, filtering what people tell us through Scripture, then pray and ask God how He'd like us to proceed.

Video devo 22 is available at www.dolifedifferent.org

Doing it different: How can you employ some upside-down (yet wise and legal) business practices in line with God's upside-down economy?

23. enjoy your work

They do not worry about how short life is, because God keeps them busy with what they love to do.
Ecclesiastes 5:20 NCV

Every year I reevaluate my priorities to make sure the needs of my family are being met. I take stock of how my kids have grown and changed and anticipate what they'll need in the coming months. I make an outline of my schedule, add school and extra-curricular activities, and then determine what I can add ... or what needs to be dropped from my commitments.

The same is true in business. We must set time aside, take stock of whether we're meeting the needs of the people we serve, and whether or not changes are needed.

King Solomon, said to be the wisest king ever, wrote the book of Ecclesiastes when contemplating the meaning of, well, life. He struggles with the meaning of life and points out all, good and bad people alike, end up the same ... dead. The end for each of us is the same. His next question is then, how can we make our time on earth meaningful?

Solomon advises his readers to slow down and enjoy what God has given. And that sentiment holds true today. Life is short. If we're to enjoy our lives, we must make time to rest, relax, and take joy in God's gifts to us, in all He has done for us. How about in your business? Are you doing what you love to do?

Take some time today to list what you love about your business, life, and family. Try to add something to your list each day this week.

Video devo 23 is available at www.dolifedifferent.org

Doing it different: Take the time to evaluate your schedule for the upcoming weeks. Will your family feel served within the current structure?

_____

_____

_____

_____

_____

24. does your business shout?

> ... lift up your voice with a shout,
> lift it up, do not be afraid; Isaiah 40:9b NIV

Not long ago, my kids and I were watching *The Chronicles of Narnia: Prince Caspian*. The prince has been looking for his father, and is convinced if he can get to Aslan's land, he can find his father. Near the end of the movie, Caspian does indeed find Aslan's land and he has to make the choice to go through or stay and lead the people of his kingdom. You see, if he goes into the land, he can't return.

Prince Caspian thinks for a moment and then decides that he will stay and lead his kingdom. He says, "I think I've spent far too long wanting what was taken from me and not being grateful for what I've been given."

That line stuck with me for a long time after the movie ended. The same thing is true in my life. I often get stuck in the past, wishing for things I feel were taken from me, instead of looking ahead grateful for what I've been given. That concept is powerful.

How about you? Are you stuck in the past? Or does your life shout out your gratefulness to your Lord and Savior?

And what about our businesses? They ought to shout out our gratefulness as well. Our customers should experience Jesus when they work with us. We should strive to be business owners that extend grace and love with each transaction.

How do we make sure our businesses (and our lives) proclaim the gospel? Gratefulness is the first step. When people see a life of gratefulness and joy, they wonder where that joy stems from. Hopefully we make people wonder, cause them to be curious about where our hope comes from. This may be just the opening we need to share our faith.

But, even if we never utter a word of the gospel to someone, our lives can reflect Christ's love. Our reputation can shout out Jesus.

Video devo 24 is available at www.dolifedifferent.org

Do Life Different

Doing it different: How can you shout gratefulness through your business in a new way?

_____
_____
_____
_____
_____
_____
_____
_____
_____
_____
_____
_____
_____
_____
_____
_____
_____

25. sometimes you gotta go for it

Those who wait for perfect weather will never plant seeds; those who look at every cloud will never harvest crops.
Ecclesiastes 11:4 NCV

Do you tend to wait for the perfect time?

Whether it's getting married, adding a child to your family, starting a business, or going back to school, many of us get in the I'll-just-wait-until-life-is-perfect mode before moving forward.

Sadly, the perfect time will never come.

I received an email from a woman not long ago asking if I thought she should start a business. She explained she had an idea she felt was from the Lord, but she also had small children and wasn't sure of the timing.

I told her that, in my experience, God never asks us to do something worthwhile when it's convenient for us. If God asks us to do something, we need to go for it. No matter what our lives look like at the time.

Do Life Different

We do, of course, need to be careful it is the Lord we're hearing from – that we're not just following our own desires. Spending time in prayer and discussing the options with our spouse or a trusted friend are important parts of making the decision to move forward.

I know those great ideas and opportunities rarely come when I'm waiting for something to do. Usually I'm in the midst of the business of life when God asks me to take up a new challenge. Sometimes that requires stepping away from other things, which can be as hard as starting something new. But, it's important we allow God's Spirit to lead us. And it's certainly more exciting when we live that way! We never know what opportunity God will bring our way next.

Don't wait for the perfect time because it will never arrive. Do listen for confirmation of God's leading. Then act.

Video devo 25 is available at www.dolifedifferent.org

Doing it different: What is on your shelf, waiting for the perfect time? Ask God if it's time to dust off that dream or idea.

26. the smallest thing

> *As one of them was cutting down a tree, the iron axhead fell into the water. "Oh no, my lord!" he cried out. "It was borrowed!" The man of God asked, "Where did it fall?" When he showed him the place, Elisha cut a stick and threw it there, and made the iron float. 2 Kings 6:5-6 NIV*

I love this story. I love that Elisha is willing to help this man with an ax. What a small thing compared to many of the other miracles in Scripture. The man borrows an ax, drops it into the water, panics and begs for help.

We all know that feeling: you borrow something from someone and lose it. Or it breaks. I can think of several times this has happened to me. I still feel that sinking in the pit of my stomach as I try to think through replacing the item or explaining what happened.

Instead of shrugging his shoulders and moving on, or deciding to use this as a life lesson for this poor man, Elisha takes the time to help him. God allows Elisha to use the power He has given him to help.

Jill Hart

I think this shows God cares about even the smallest things in our lives.

It's so easy to overlook the small miracles that God does. You hear just the song you needed. You lose keys and cry out to God and ... there they are.

But, wouldn't you agree sometimes the small things in life we need to be the most aware of?

God cares about job loss, financial struggles, and health issues. God sees. And He cares. One of the very names of God reflects this aspect of His character. El Roi. Literally, "The God Who Sees Me."

Hagar attributes this name to God when He rescues her in the wilderness, after she runs away from an angry Sarah and after conceiving a son with Abraham (at Sarah's insistence). The angel of the Lord visits Hagar in the desert, encouraging her to return to her mistress and prophesying over her unborn child.

Hagar, who thought she was alone and abandoned; who thought no one could see her when she was mistreated, now knows that God Almighty sees her – and knows her by name!

And He sees you. God knows you by name.

Video devo 26 is available at www.dolifedifferent.org

Do Life Different

Doing it different: What seemingly small things are you carrying alone right now? Write them down, then pray a prayer of surrender to God.

_____
_____
_____
_____
_____
_____
_____
_____
_____
_____
_____
_____
_____
_____
_____
_____
_____

27. better late than never

Then the Lord said to Joshua, "Do not be afraid; do not be discouraged. Take the whole army with you, and go up and attack Ai. For I have delivered into your hands the king of Ai, his people, his city and his land." Joshua 8:1 NIV

After Jericho, God tells the Israelites that it's time to move to the next town, Ai, to defeat them as well. God gives them specific rules once they defeated Jericho, namely not to take any possessions from Jericho as their own. However, unbeknownst to Joshua, someone does take spoils and hides them.

So, the Israelites move forward and attack Ai. And they are defeated.

Joshua and the Israelite leaders are stunned. They don't understand. What happened? Joshua falls on his face before God, frustrated and asking why God would bring them into the Promised Land just to allow them to die.

Do Life Different

God then reveals the deceit of Achan. The Israelites repent and handle the situation as God asks. The Lord gives them a second chance, and they defeat Ai.

This story so pointedly reminds us that victory and success come completely from the Lord. They have nothing to do with us and can be taken away in an instant. Every talent, skill, ability is completely a gift from God.

Like the Israelites, we too can become prideful when we see success in our lives. We expect God to continue our success. That's often the time sin has crept into our lives, not only in pride and arrogance, but actions we know do not please God. Maybe we think He won't notice or somehow won't mind just this one time.

The beauty of this story, though, is the message that we can go to God when we mess up. Through wholehearted repentance, we receive His forgiveness. And then we can try again. And again. And sometimes a fourth or fifth time, too.

None of the things we do (or don't do) make God love us less or more. He is faithful and will continue to forgive and give us another chance.

Video devo 27 is available at www.dolifedifferent.org

Doing it different: Is there an area of your life that needs to be confessed and changed? If so, spend some time on your knees before God today restoring your relationship and receiving His never-ending forgiveness and grace.

Do Life Different

28. what will you choose?

The word of the LORD came to Jonah son of Amittai: "Go to the great city of Nineveh and preach against it, because its wickedness has come up before me." But Jonah ran away from the LORD and headed for Tarshish. Jonah 1:1-3a NIV

Recently I was asked to do something I didn't want to do. I said no. But the request kept bothering me at the most unexpected times—in the shower, at the grocery store, in the middle of the night. Finally, after God repeatedly brought it to mind (and I lost several nights sleep), I realized He wanted me to act. In obedience, I had to go tell the person yes. Only then did I get a good night's rest.

Not long after, I was reading through the Old Testament and came to the book of Jonah. As I read through the first chapter of his story, I realized Jonah and I had a lot in common.

If God asks something I don't want to do, I simply don't do it. I may not get on a boat headed the opposite direction, like Jonah did. But, it took several nights of lost sleep and nagging thoughts before I was willing to concede my wrongdoing.

Of course, sometimes it's not something we don't want to do. Sometimes it's simply not in the plan we've drawn for our lives. We have an idea of what we want our life to look like and don't leave a lot of room for divine detours.

The redeeming quality of this story is that God pursued Jonah all the way out to sea and beyond. He let Jonah run. But he pursued, not to capture, but to allow a change of heart and mind. He could have forced His will, but, instead, He waited for the consequences to turn people back to Him.

Isn't it reassuring to know God will pursue us even when we're in the wrong and running from Him? He gently pursued me and waited until I was willing to do as He asked. Looking back, I'm very glad I did.

What do you do when God asks something you don't want to do? Do you run away? Or do you walk forward in obedience?

Is there an area in your life where you need to set aside fear and do what God is asking? Do you need to set aside your own agenda and do His will?

Do Life Different

God knows what's best for us. He loves to use the unexpected to refine and challenge us.

Video devo 28 is available at www.dolifedifferent.org

Doing it different: Can you objectively see a similar scenario playing out in a friend's life? Spend time over a coffee talking about your goals and pray for direction. His direction. Then encourage one another to act.

Jill Hart

29. the God who wastes nothing

At this the men greatly feared the Lord, and they offered a sacrifice to the Lord and made vows to him. Jonah 1:16 NIV

I think one of the things I appreciate most about God is that He never wastes an experience. When I look back over my life, I can see how He's shaped and molded each season to bring me right where I am. My family, schooling, and different jobs I've held—I can see God's design in it all. He's molding me right now for what's next.

We can see this same principle hold true in another piece of Jonah's story. Jonah is on the boat, headed in the opposite direction from God's direction. He's sound asleep in the belly of the ship, but raging around him is a huge storm.

The sailors are thrown into a panic, tossing cargo from the ship left and right. They call on all of the gods they know and doing everything to lighten the ship and stay afloat.

Do Life Different

Eventually, they cast lots and determine Jonah is at fault. He owns up to it and tells them to throw him over. The sailors keep trying to lighten the ship and even try rowing back to land. Nothing works.

Finally, out of sheer desperation, the sailors cry out to God and ask Him not to punish them for Jonah's death and to throw him overboard, " ... and the raging sea grew calm."

God, in His infinite wisdom wastes nothing from Jonah's life, even his disobedience:

"At this the men greatly feared the Lord, and they offered a sacrifice to the Lord and made vows to him."

God uses Jonah's disobedience to lead these sailors to worship Him. In the midst of disciplining Jonah for running away, God is still concerned about the other men's hearts.

Have you seen this happen? When you look back over your experiences, can you see God's hand guiding and directing?

Video devo 29 is available at www.dolifedifferent.org

Doing it different: How has God used your mistake for His glory and your growth? Have you told anyone about it? Be willing to humble yourself by being honest about your growth process. Someone else may be touched by the situation.

30. God uses nobodies

After this the Lord appointed seventy-two others and sent them two by two ahead of him to every town and place where he was about to go. Luke 10:1 NIV

God can use me. Though Jesus had twelve disciples who were closest to him, he also had many, many followers He discipled as well. The leadership training went primarily to the twelve, but Jesus did choose others.

In Luke, Jesus sent out seventy-two people to share the good news. *Jesus is the Son of God.* They prepared the way for Jesus to go into towns and reach as many people as possible.

We don't know background info or education levels. We don't know where they were from or their names. They were, in essence, nobodies just like you and me.

I don't know about you, but I often question if God can really use me. I'm not smart enough, thin enough, pretty enough, to do what God asks of me. I don't have a fancy-enough degree. I can't sing or play the piano. All silly ideas when said out loud, but things that seem true enough to disqualify me in my head.

However, none of that matters to God. He uses whomever He chooses: big or small, tall or short, pretty or plain, and in-between. God confirms this in His Word:

The Lord does not look at the things people look at. People look at the outward appearance, but the Lord looks at the heart." 1 Samuel 16: 7b

We can be used of God just as we are. No matter what our dreams are, no matter what our accomplishments are, no matter what our skills may be.

He doesn't choose just the best and the brightest. He uses the weak to lead the strong (1 Corinthians 1:27).

He'll use you no matter who you are, no matter what you have, or don't have, going for you.

Video devo 30 is available at www.dolifedifferent.org

Do Life Different

Doing it different: Have you felt disqualified from being used by God? What areas of your life have brought you insecurity? How can you reframe those things about yourself and make them positive for Kingdom purposes?

_____
_____
_____
_____
_____
_____
_____
_____
_____
_____
_____
_____
_____
_____

Jill Hart

31. what if God has bigger plans for you?

In their hearts humans plan their course, but the Lord establishes their steps. Proverbs 16:9 NIV

What did you want to be when you grew up? For many years my daughter told everyone that she was going to be a face painter. I laughed at the expressions every time she told someone. She changed her mind and currently plans on being a chef or a missionary — much better choices in this momma's opinion.

When I began working from home, I thought I wanted to be a web designer. I started learning to build websites. CWAHM was the first in a series of websites I planned to develop a portfolio.

I wasn't very good at building websites. I wouldn't want to show you what the first (or second or third) version of CWAHM looked like. Thankfully, God had another plan.

We think we know what our future holds, or where we're heading. We have a goal and a plan in mind and we race through life as if we are in control. I talk with women all the time who've headed down one road when God drastically alters their course.

Sometimes it's illness; sometimes it's divorce; sometimes it's a job change or geographical move.

We never know when God might decide to change our lives. He often uses hard circumstances or even places of fear to challenge and grow us.

In college, we were required to take Speech class. I was terrified of speaking in front of people, so I took the course at our local community college during summer session instead of the college I attended. I figured I wouldn't have to see any of the people ever again.

The irony is that God developed my speaking ministry out of what He's doing at CWAHM. Now I speak in front of large crowds—and enjoy it. God has such a different plan than I'd ever imagined.

I've had to lay down many dreams and plans. But God's plans are always so much better than anything I could dream. I wouldn't want it any other way.

Video devo 31 is available at www.dolifedifferent.org

Jill Hart

Doing it different: Are there places where God wants to broaden your horizons? What might He have planned if you abandon yourself to God?

32. finding your hidden talents

For you created my inmost being; you knit me together in my mother's womb. Psalm 139:13 NIV

What a miracle it is that any of us exist. The fact you exist on this planet at all means God knit you together. He designed you and He has a plan for your life (see Jeremiah 29:11). You were created for a purpose.

I know many days it may not feel like you have a special talent or purpose to offer.

Growing up I was never the *best* at anything. I took piano lessons and was passably good, but not great. I played soccer in junior high and high school, but was pretty awful. I tried some different clubs and groups throughout high school and college, but never found that *one thing* where I could stand out.

I could describe myself as someone who spent time figuring out how to blend into the crowd better. For the most part, I was okay with being average. I thought I would live a normal life—husband, kids, job—and that would be it. I had no idea God had a PLAN for my life, that I could be useful to Him, and serve others to glorify God.

Part of God's calling on my life is as a wife and mother. Another is as a business owner, writer, and speaker. Owning a business is not something I thought I'd ever do, nor did I have any desire to be a writer or a speaker.

However, as we walk forward in our calling, being obedient to what God has asked, He'll begin to reveal things about ourselves we aren't aware of. I had no idea writing would be a part of my life until CWAHM began to grow and need content. Who else was there to write it but me? So, I wrote. God blessed that obedience by providing many writing opportunities throughout the years.

God gave you unique skills and talents for a purpose. You have something to offer – it just may not be what you expected.

Look at where you're at right now, objectively, as a business owner. Does anything stand out? Maybe you're a great communicator. Maybe you excel at coaching the members of your business team. Or maybe you've noticed God has given you talent as a writer, artist, or in another area. What brings you joy?

Do Life Different

What feels right? See what God may be doing within you and through you.

Video devo 32 is available at www.dolifedifferent.org

Doing it different: Step out in faith in a new area of business or ministry. Accept the request to speak, take on that big client, or start a class. Be open to the new thing God wants to develop.

_____
_____
_____
_____
_____
_____
_____
_____
_____
_____
_____
_____
_____
_____

33. doing It God's way

> *Do not deceive yourselves. If any of you think you are wise by the standards of this age, you should become "fools" so that you may become wise. For the wisdom of this world is foolishness in God's sight. As it is written: "He catches the wise in their craftiness." 1 Corinthians 3:18-19 NIV*

Our ways are not God's ways.

Successful people do things a certain way. They follow proven business principles. Logic tells us to mimic their behaviors and expect their results, but nothing seems to work for us.

Their way of running a business often runs counter to how God asks us to handle things. God's ways may appear strange, even illogical at times, but they always work because of who He is: faithful and true. Expert wisdom, practiced in our lives, may be foolishness in the eyes of God.

For example, God's Word tells us that when we give, getting from God is the natural by-product (Luke

6:38). This is in opposition to what is taught in business school. Marketers yell, "Look out for number one!" Spend on number one. Save for number one.

We don't have to do business the same way even though their tactics may seem to work. We are to rely on godly business practices, trusting God to handle the rest.

While the world tells us to build a social media voice, market a brand, and create a platform, we can rest in knowing God has a plan for us and will bring opportunities our way.

For example, over the last couple of years I've been building the speaking part of my ministry. I worked and pushed and fussed at myself because I couldn't make all the things happen I hoped. I finally surrendered it to God and asked Him to bring me the opportunities He wanted me to have.

And guess what? That's exactly what He's done.

When it comes right down to it, what's important in our businesses, and in our entire lives, is that we do things God's way.

Video devo 33 is available at www.dolifedifferent.org

Doing it different: How are you doing business? Marriage? Parenthood? Are you following the world, the way everyone else does those things? How could you alter your practices to line up with God's way?

34. when we are weak

Therefore, in order to keep me from becoming conceited, I was given a thorn in my flesh, a messenger of Satan, to torment me. Three times I pleaded with the Lord to take it away from me. But he said to me, "My grace is sufficient for you, for my power is made perfect in weakness."

Therefore I will boast all the more gladly about my weaknesses, so that Christ's power may rest on me. That is why, for Christ's sake, I delight in weaknesses, in insults, in hardships, in persecutions, in difficulties. For when I am weak, then I am strong. 2 Corinthians 12:7b-10 NIV

For the past few years, I've been struggling with my thyroid. I have Grave's Disease and trying to get it leveled out has been a torturous up-and-down process. Each medicinal change takes several weeks (or months) to determine effectiveness. And then we have to adjust things again. It can be pretty frustrating and discouraging.

God why do I have to deal with this? Don't You know I have things to do and places to go? (Wink.)

The apostle Paul points out sometimes we're given issues to keep us humble. God knows we love to be in control. When everything is peachy, we tend to rely on ourselves instead of on Him.

And when we succeed—building a business or raising a family—all glory needs to go to the Lord. We must be careful we don't become boastful or conceited. When we begin to think we've really done something, that the good accomplishment is anything other than the grace and mercy of God, we're headed for trouble.

It's so easy to become prideful and think we know what we're doing. When this happens, I tend to brush aside my quiet time with the Lord thinking, *I'm much too busy to fit that in today.* As I draw away from God, and begin to rely on self, can you guess what happens?

I end up flat on my face, having made a mess of the situation. I can't tell you how many times I've had to learn this lesson the hard way.

Our trust and security must be firmly rooted in our heavenly Father. All glory and honor belong to Him and Him alone.

Do Life Different

Video devo 34 is available at www.dolifedifferent.org

Doing it different: Have you been trusting God in your weakness? Or are you feeling strong and trying to handle things your own way? Does a friend need support in a similar discovery?

35. feeling restless

So I say, walk by the Spirit, and you will not gratify the desires of the flesh. For the flesh desires what is contrary to the Spirit, and the Spirit what is contrary to the flesh. They are in conflict with each other, so that you are not to do whatever you want. But if you are led by the Spirit, you are not under the law. Galatians 5:16-18 NIV

Lately I've felt restless. Like something isn't quite right. I needed a change, but I wasn't quite sure where to start or to do.

Do you ever feel that way?

When coaching clients feel this way, I like to ask, "If you could do anything differently in your life right now, what would you do?" Based on the answer, we can determine what change needs to be made, and set goals to work toward.

We *should* feel that something-needs-to-change nudge because of the war between our sinful wants

Do Life Different

and the Holy Spirit's conviction. There's a constant battle between what *we* want and what *God* wants.

The line from these verses that stands out to me the most is, "so that you are not to do whatever you want." Ouch! None of us wants to hear that.

As Christ followers, we don't get to do what we please. We are called to be like Christ. Our goal is to love the Lord and to love others the way He does.

It's not at all about what you or I want.

Many days it feels like an impossible reality. How can I, a sinful, pitiful mess, ever be like Christ?

The beauty? It's the Spirit within us that works to make us like Him. When we listen and obey the Spirit's promptings we'll become more Christ-like. We can't do it in our own power. I find freedom in that fact.

Video devo 35 is available at www.dolifedifferent.org

Doing it different: Is God calling you to change today? What attitudes or behaviors do you need to submit to Him?

Jill Hart

36. made for a special purpose

In a large house there are not only things made of gold and silver, but also things made of wood and clay. Some things are used for special purposes, and others are made for ordinary jobs. All who make themselves clean from evil will be used for special purposes. They will be made holy, useful to the Master, ready to do any good work.
2 Timothy 2:20-21 NCV

Have you ever felt like your life isn't as important as other people's lives? As if God created others to do big things, but He created you for a boring life?

2 Timothy paints the picture of God as the potter. He creates certain pots for special purposes and others for common use.

I've always stopped at that first verse because it sounded depressing. I must not be one of the lucky ones God had created for some amazing purpose. A common cup with a common purpose.

But the next verse begins with the word "All."

Read it again: "All who make themselves clean from evil will be used for special purposes."

Do you see it? *Any of us* can be made useful for Him. That's exciting! That's life changing!

By obedience to God, we "make ourselves clean" through repenting and believing God, and we can be used for special purposes. Notice it doesn't say, "All those ... might be used." But we *will* be used for special purposes—that's a promise!

We need to grasp this. We need to believe what God says here. When we are obedient to Him, He will use us.

How do we "make ourselves clean?" First and foremost, this is a call to salvation. We place our trust in Jesus, His death on the cross, and His victory over the grave. We confess our sinful state to God and place our lives in His hands.

And secondly, we are also called to *do* something. When we are saved, we receive the Holy Spirit and are set free from the bondage to sin. That means it's now within our power, through the Holy Spirit, to flee from evil. We set aside the sin that held us captive before we knew God.

Does this mean we need to be perfect? No. God knows we are still sinful human beings. What it does

Do Life Different

mean is that our hearts now seek Him above all else. And the promise says we will be used by God.

Video devo 36 is available at www.dolifedifferent.org

Doing it different: Have you received Christ as your Savior? Are you ready to be used by Him? Ask Him to cleanse you and use you.

_____
_____
_____
_____
_____
_____
_____
_____
_____
_____
_____
_____

37. when we are struggling

Not only so, but we also glory in our sufferings, because we know that suffering produces perseverance; perseverance, character; and character, hope. And hope does not put us to shame, because God's love has been poured out into our hearts through the Holy Spirit, who has been given to us.
Romans 5:3-5 NIV

Okay, I admit it. I struggle with fear. Fear of failure. Fear of loss. Fear of the unknown. It seems like there is always something lurking around the corner I feel the need to worry about. And somehow I've convinced myself that worry is a proactive pursuit. Because I'm worrying then it can't happen. I think we all know that is not the case.

We'll have struggles, issues, hurts. There's just no way around it. We can worry all we like, but worry will never solve the problem or take away the struggle.

Only relying on Christ, the Prince of Peace, can bring true peace and even joy into the midst of even the most difficult circumstances.

When my husband's job was on the line because of budget cuts, God challenged me in this area. I wanted to find a job at the nearest department store and try to fix the problem myself. But I felt God asking me to relax and trust Him.

It's so easy to say to someone else, "Just trust God." It's so much harder to live it.

But God is faithful, and He provided for us during our time of uncertainty in ways I'd never believe had I not seen it happen. While I had to be thrifty, we always had just enough money to pay the bills. When my kids needed new clothing or school supplies, God provided through others unexpectedly. He spoiled us with little gifts we might have overlooked. But during this time the gifts were sweet reminders He was caring for us.

Often it's when we struggle that we cling to God the most. He uses these times to build our dependence on Him and to refine us into women who more clearly reflect His character.

Video devo 37 is available at www.dolifedifferent.org

Doing it different: What worries do you need to lay at His feet today? Can you trust Him with the unknown?

38. living in abundance

I have come that they may have life, and have it to the full.
John 10:10b NIV

I thought I'd grow up, get married, have kids, have a career and life would be peaches and roses. I daydreamed about getting married. I dreamed of the children who'd listen and obey without ever misbehaving. I saw myself gliding happily through life without a care in the world.

Hopefully you're smiling by now, realizing my reality hasn't quite matched up to what I imagined. My husband and children are wonderful, but they certainly aren't perfect and we all tend to get on each other's nerves once in a while. Don't even get me started on bills.

In John 10:10, Jesus tells us that He is the one who brings life — *full* life.

When you think about "a full life," what does that mean to you? Is it possessions? Wealth? I don't think that's what Jesus means.

A full, abundant, life is so much *more* than possessions or money or success. God's economy and His business tactics are totally different from the worlds. It's upside down compared to what we're told to want out of life. The world tells us we need a nice house, a fancy car, and perfect kids in order to be happy and feel successful.

But there's much more to life than that.

The abundant life is all about walking closely with God, knowing Him intimately. It's about getting to do God's work.

I came to the realization that I don't want to live half a life. I don't want to be so concerned with my own selfish needs that I miss the needs of others around me. I don't want to be so focused on obtaining the trappings of this world that I miss the amazing gift of knowing the God of the universe. That He even notices us should cause us to pause in wonder every day.

Having perfect children or a perfect business or a perfect spouse, all of the right things—none of those bring happiness or abundant life. We can look at the

Do Life Different

lives of wealthy Hollywood stars and see that money and fame aren't what bring happiness.

Only Jesus can bring abundance to your life. Only He can create love overflowing within you.

Video devo 38 is available at www.dolifedifferent.org

Doing it different: Are you living an abundant life? If not, what changes do you need to make?

_____

_____

_____

_____

_____

_____

_____

_____

_____

_____

_____

_____

Jill Hart

39. working through the impossible

Against all hope, Abraham in hope believed and so became the father of many nations, just as it had been said to him, "So shall your offspring be." Without weakening in his faith, he faced the fact that his body was as good as dead—since he was about a hundred years old—and that Sarah's womb was also dead. Yet he did not waver through unbelief regarding the promise of God, but was strengthened in his faith and gave glory to God, being fully persuaded that God had power to do what he had promised.
Romans 4:18-21 NIV

I love the first three words of that verse, "Against all hope." God promised Abraham would be the father of many nations. As Abraham and his wife, Sarah, grew older it became less and less likely that their human bodies would be able to produce offspring.

Even in the midst of what seemed impossible, Abraham believed God. Abraham was fully aware that what he was hoping for was not possible: "… *he*

Do Life Different

faced the fact that his body was as good as dead — since he was about a hundred years old — and that Sarah's womb was also dead." Abraham knew that however God chose to grant him a son, it'd be miraculous. He still chose to believe God would act on his promise.

Abraham was right with God because of this type of faith. He believed against all hope.

Do you believe God will do what He says even when circumstances look bleak?

I have a hard time waiting. I hate to wait in line or in traffic. I get antsy when I'm waiting for God to move in the circumstances surrounding me. I'm rarely steady enough in my faith to trust God without being filled with doubts and what-ifs.

It's easy to forget God already knows what we're going to face. He's not taken by surprise when we lose a job, are diagnosed with an illness, or face the death of a loved one. He's not thrown off when our finances are a mess. He's not worried when a curve ball comes our way.

He knows things will look impossible from our angle. He wants us to trust Him even then. Against all hope.

When we choose to trust God, even in the midst of impossible odds, that's when God often chooses to move in miraculous ways. He blessed 90-year-old Abraham with a son. God can work miracles in your life, too. The key is to trust Him no matter how long it takes, no matter how bleak it looks.

Video devo 39 is available at www.dolifedifferent.org

Doing it different: What do you need to trust God with today? Think of how you normally handle those situations. Identify some ways you can show more trust in God?

_____
_____
_____
_____
_____
_____
_____
_____
_____
_____
_____

40. seeing the leader within

... if it is to lead, do it diligently; if it is to show mercy, do it cheerfully. Romans 12:8b NIV

I ran my website, www.CWAHM.com, for many years before I saw myself as a leader. In my mind, I was just a mommy blogger trying to work from home. After I'd been in business for nearly ten years, a good friend and mentor sat me down and challenged me to begin acting like a leader. She told me that women were looking to me not only for help in working from home, but for advice on parenting, spiritual growth, and other areas of life.

I tried to deny I was leader because the title scared me. It still does. When I think of a leader, I think of my pastor or government officials. Leadership comes with responsibility, and I wasn't sure I was willing to take that on.

As I prayed about this idea of being a leader, God showed me He'd already put me a in a place of leadership. I could step into that role or step back into the comfort of a normal life.

Many of us don't want to accept when God calls us into ministry or leadership. Realize, however, that you're likely already a leader in some form. If you're a mom, you're a leader. If you help with the children at church, you're a leader. If you're a Christian, you're a leader. People are watching you live and represent Christ. If you don't believe me, ask God to show you who you might be leading.

Stepping out of our comfort zone can be scary and sometimes painful. Moving from an unintentional leader to an *intentional* (or diligent) leader may feel like a big jump, but the rewards are eternal.

Once you begin to see yourself as a leader, you will begin to act like a leader so you don't end up incompetent. No one sets out to be a bad leader, but if you aren't being intentional, then you've set yourself up for failure.

Lead your children. Lead at church. You may not know it, but people look up to you. Instead of sticking your head in the sand and telling yourself you could never be a leader, ask God what He has for you. Be willing to step forward and lead the people who look to you.

Do Life Different

Video devo 40 is available at www.dolifedifferent.org

Doing it different: Describe your leadership style. If you don't know, read a book on leadership. Now name one way you can be a more intentional leader at church, at home, and in the community.

_____
_____
_____
_____
_____
_____
_____
_____
_____
_____
_____
_____
_____

41. is success okay?

Be careful that you do not forget the LORD your God, failing to observe his commands, his laws and his decrees that I am giving you this day. Deuteronomy 8:11 NIV

The discipleship pastor at our church asked, "Jill, what do you see as some of the major struggles of the women who connect with you through CWAHM?"

As I thought about it, I realized the questions a great many women in business ask are things like:

Is it okay to be successful?

Is it okay if God allows me to succeed and not someone else?

Is it okay for me to want to succeed?

As Christians, we sometimes have the mindset we need to struggle in order to grow in our faith. And it's true our faith is stretched and refined during the difficult times. It's these hard experiences that test our characters.

So when we see abundance and success, sometimes we panic. We're afraid pride will take over. Or we're afraid God is setting us up for heartache on the other side of the success. We don't trust that success can be in His plan for us.

I expressed this to my pastor.

He said something that put it all into perspective for me. "It's all about the heart, isn't it?"

He's so right. It's all about where our heart is, what our heart is focused on.

If our heart is right, finances and success won't be the most important thing in our lives. Money and power won't be idols. If our hearts are right, success is welcome because our eyes are fixed on Christ and we're praising Him no matter what happens around us.

In our final days, we'll be much more concerned about whether or not our hearts are right with God, not whether we were successful in life.

We are to be humble before God, recognizing all God has done in us, for us, and through us.

Video devo 41 is available at www.dolifedifferent.org

Jill Hart

Doing it different: How have you hindered success to protect your sense of humility? How can you embrace anew what you have withheld? Do you know a friend who needs this message?

42. how to balance it all

Trust in the LORD with all your heart and lean not on your own understanding; in all your ways submit to him, and he will make your paths straight. Proverb 3:5-6 NIV

There are so many days when I live with a sense of guilt. I feel guilty working because I want to be with my kids (especially in the summer), but then I feel guilty when I'm with my kids because I should be working. Do you ever experience this?

I've made it all about me. I'm constantly telling myself what I should be doing – and it never seems to match what I'm doing at that moment. So, I can never measure up in my mind.

The key? I shift my focus to what God is asking, not what I think I should be doing. He may be asking me to split time between the business He's given me and the children He's blessed me with. And that's okay. What's not okay is letting the tug-of-war rise up in my conscience.

I need to spend time with my kids trusting it's where God wants me at that moment. I need to work as if I'm doing what I'm called to do at that particular time. Present in that moment. When I try to figure it all out, plan it down to the millisecond, or guilt-trip myself, that makes my kids and I miserable.

We are to trust God and His plans for us. This can be so hard to live out. Leaning not on my understanding is tough because I think I know it all. Subconsciously, I believe I can handle things, and I end up placing my trust in my ideas rather than in the Lord.

This can also mean *not* doing things. I've learned that I'm not to work first thing in the morning. I need to start the day off with God, and if I don't, it generally doesn't happen at all. Many mornings I wake up with a project I want to tackle. I have to remind myself to put it off until after my time with God.

When we start our day off in His word, we're calmer and less stressed. God's presence brings us peace and allows us to begin our day with a fresh perspective and with His leading.

No matter how busy the day ahead, we can trust Him to guide us and bring the tasks we need to accomplish and the people we need to minister to. It

Do Life Different

may not look like we expect, but His way is always better in the end.

Video devo 42 is available at www.dolifedifferent.org

Doing it different: What are some practical ways you can compartmentalize your tasks so you're present in each moment? Consider discussing this with a believing friend or group.

_____
_____
_____
_____
_____
_____
_____
_____
_____
_____
_____
_____

43. what's your goal?

Let love be your highest goal! 1 Corinthians 14:1a NLT

As a business coach, I start new clients by guiding them to set goals. That helps us find our direction and plot achievable, measureable steps to meet the goals for themselves and for their businesses.

Once we have a goal, it's much easier to make a plan.

If we're running our businesses and our lives without any goals, we're headed nowhere. We'll flail around trying to grab whatever new idea comes our way. When we set goals, we can filter new ideas and opportunities through the lens of those goals. If the steps match our goals, we can feel confident walking forward.

However, we must remember to be sensitive to God's leading. He may allow changes to alter our route. We may know where we're headed, but He may have another plan.

Do Life Different

When we're flexible, we trust that God's plan is greater than ours. I can say from personal experience the plans that come straight from God are always better than those I come up with.

In the verse above, we see the apostle Paul's life goal: love. In the chapter prior and the passage after it, Paul explains spiritual gifts. He stops in the middle of talking about the gifts of the Spirit to remind the reader to, "Let love be your highest goal."

Paul knew his audience was excited about the spiritual gifts that God bestows on His people. He saw people becoming more focused on their gifts than on loving one another. He knew they needed a reminder that love is far more important than any spiritual gift we can receive.

The same is true when applied to business. It's easy to get wrapped up and miss the relationships and people around us. When we take time to listen to a hurting friend or reach out to a new neighbor, despite our busy schedules, that's making love our highest goal. When we take time out of our busy schedules to love one another, that's when we're showing Christ-like love.

Video devo 43 is available at www.dolifedifferent.org

Doing it different: Are you wrapped up in your business or your busy-ness? Who can you reach out to today in love? Is there a relationship or a need you've missed? What can you do about that now?

44. get off your duff

Look at the birds of the air; they do not sow or reap or store away in barns, and yet your heavenly Father feeds them. Are you not much more valuable than they?
Matthew 6:26 NIV

I heard a quote that challenged me. Author Andy Andrews said, "Yes, God does feed the birds of the air, but He's not throwing the worms into their nests."

Doesn't that make you stop and think?

God promises to provide for us, but work is required on our part. Just like birds have to build nests and search for worms, we must do the work God has called us to do during our time here on Earth.

I think there's a delicate balance figuring out what part we are to do and what part we are to let God handle. Many times being out of balance is caused by our need to be in control. If we're working because we feel we know best or we need to be in control, there comes a time when God will ask us to hand it to Him and trust Him with it.

But, like the birds, some things are our responsibility. God is not going to do the laundry for me.

Working from home takes effort. Raising godly children takes effort. A great marriage takes effort. The worthwhile things in life won't often be thrown into your nest.

During my years working from home, many opportunities have come my way as blessings from God. Other opportunities have come as a result of work He has asked me to do. Had I not done the work, I wouldn't have come across that opportunity.

As much as we're to "Let go and let God," we're also called to obey and do what He asks. It's when we find the balance between the two – letting God handle the things that are His, and doing the work that is ours – we find contentment and peace.

This can be a hard balance to find. It's a life-long journey. However, we're in good hands as we trust God to lead and guide us every step of the way.

Video devo 44 is available at www.dolifedifferent.org.

Do Life Different

Doing it different: What do you need to let go of and give to God? What work are you feeling called forward in?

_____

_____

_____

_____

_____

_____

_____

_____

_____

_____

_____

_____

_____

_____

45. the act of starting

> *David also said to Solomon his son, "Be strong and courageous, and do the work. Do not be afraid or discouraged, for the Lord God, my God, is with you.*
> *1 Chronicles 28:20b NIV*

Countless women have asked how it's possible to start working from home. My reply is, "Pick something and start." The act of starting something new is often the hardest step of all.

When I began working from home, I did data entry for a local company. It wasn't my dream job, and it wasn't what I was going to do long-term, but it took me where I needed to be – home. Once comfortable with that job and doing it well, I began learning to build websites during my off-hours. I designed CWAHM during those days, thinking it'd be a neat project and something I could show customers.

God had other plans for CWAHM, but I'd never have progressed that far had I not stepped out in faith toward what I felt God asking – quitting my full-time corporate job and work at home entering data. I had to work hard at a job that paid very little for a while, but I learned the ropes of working from home: perseverance, determination, and communication. That led me to what God had for me next.

If you're facing a challenge, something you aren't sure how to start, begin by breaking it down into manageable action steps. Make a to-do list of each step. Then take each of those items and break them down into as many steps as necessary to accomplish the project.

Once you have your list complete, challenge yourself. Pick the hardest thing on your to-do list you can do now and get it done. Once you have that completed, you'll gain confidence to take on anything.

Take that step of faith today and get started. Whether God is calling you to something that seems huge – like starting a business or finding a work-at-home job – or talking to your spouse about your desire to work from home, it's time to move forward.

Taking that first step can be extremely hard, but once the first step behind you the next is often easier. Ask God to guide your steps and timing, allowing the peace of mind that you're doing what He has called you to do.

Jill Hart

Video devo 45 is available at www.dolifedifferent.org.

Doing it different: What is your ultimate goal for your work-at-home endeavors? What's the very next step? What's preventing you from taking that step right now?

46. all talk

All hard work brings a profit, but mere talk leads only to poverty. Proverbs 14:23 NIV

I cringe every time I read this verse because of the amount of truth packed into this small sentence. I've seen this concept played out time and time again. I come up with what I believe is a really good idea, but I let fear stop me from moving forward and accomplishing it.

I believe this holds true in every area of our lives:

When we work hard, we see a profit (no matter how small). When we talk, without action, there isn't even a chance to see a profit because nothing actually gets done.

In relationships we see the results (profits) from that hard work in love, trust, and friendship. If all we do is talk about how we'd like our relationships to be, we'll never see them change.

I started thinking about where my life is right now. What am I *all-talk* about? What is *all-talk* in your life?

Let this verse be our call to action. Let's move forward with a renewed sense of purpose. Resolve to change your *all-talk* into *all-do*. Pick up the phone and reach out to a loved one. Set aside distraction-free time with your children. Say something loving and encouraging to your spouse. Have your daily quiet times.

Decide to take the first step toward the goal you'd like to see profit in. Don't let fear, unforgiveness, or bitterness stand in your way. Don't be afraid to take a chance and do the work necessary to mend that broken relationship or start that new business idea you've been thinking about for a while.

Put forth effort, and trust the results to God. You're bound to be surprised by all that can be accomplished.

Video devo 46 is available at www.dolifedifferent.org.

Do Life Different

Doing it different: How can you turn that big *all-talk* issue into an *all-do* action?

_____
_____
_____
_____
_____
_____
_____
_____
_____
_____
_____
_____
_____
_____
_____
_____
_____

47. appearances

> *But the Lord said to Samuel, "Do not consider his appearance or his height, for I have rejected him. The Lord does not look at the things people look at. People look at the outward appearance, but the Lord looks at the heart." 1 Samuel 16:7 NIV*

When I first started out in business, I wanted people to think I was successful. I went out of my way to appear that way to others. If I looked accomplished on the outside, people would treat me as successful, and that would somehow help me become so in truth.

I wasn't completely wrong. I do believe we need to present ourselves confidently to others, especially if we're stepping out in faith as God has asked. However, when we're content to stop with appearances we find ourselves in trouble.

When my daughter started kindergarten I took my place in the line of parents to pick her up. In that line day after day, noticed all the minivans, and my car no longer measured up. I believed these moms wouldn't accept me unless I drove a minivan, too.

Over the next couple of months I managed to talk my husband into getting a minivan. I hated it. It felt like driving a bus. I parked near the far edge of any parking lot because I was so ridiculously bad at parking the thing.

Many of you probably drive minivans, and that's completely fine, but my minivan became some sort of status symbol gone wrong. It wreaked havoc on my life. What I thought would bring me acceptance actually brought me annoyance and frustration. I struggled to drive it and we struggled to make the payment each month.

I learned a hard lesson through that minivan. I can't base my self-worth on what I drive – or wear, or weigh …

God certainly doesn't judge us based on any of these human measures of self-worth. God sees our hearts and knows who seeks Him. He doesn't care what we look like. He doesn't care about any of the worldly things we so easily become entangled in. Only when we pursue Him above all else will we find true acceptance.

Jill Hart

Video devo 47 is available at www.dolifedifferent.org.

Doing it different: What are you basing your self-worth on? Do you have a status-symbol-gone-wrong? How can you rectify that mistake?

48. choosing joy

Rejoice in the Lord always. I will say it again: Rejoice!
Philippians 4:4 NIV

Our pastor gave a sermon on the topic of joy. I like to consider myself a joyful person, but his words challenged me. He reminded us joy is not only a spiritual fruit (Gal 5:22), but it is also a command.

When God talks about joy in His Word, He's generally telling us to choose it.

It doesn't say look for joy, hope for joy, or rejoice when things are great. It says rejoice *always*. How does one go about choosing to be joyful always?

I'm a worrywart. I struggle with fear and worry, sometimes wide-awake in the middle of the night fretting. But this verse calls us to rejoice even when life is rough. Right after a diagnosis of thyroid disease, I wasn't in a place to rejoice about it. But, as the months went on, and I saw God working in new ways, I did realize pieces I could rejoice in. I also began rejoicing about the little things I take for granted when all is well: time with my kids, the sound of rain, a deep breath after waking up in the morning.

God changed me through the experience. I found myself praying, "Thank you for taking me through this. Thank you for this opportunity to trust you."

In his sermon, our pastor said, "Struggles are postcards from God where we get to see His provision in our lives."

When times are tough, we turn to God. When struggling is a part of daily existence, it feels natural be much more dependent on God and much more willing to seek His help. Each time we see God's provision and answer to our prayers, it's like receiving a postcard letting us know how much He truly cares for us.

We can rejoice because He cares for us and will see us through. Every struggle is an opportunity to know God more.

Video devo 48 is available at www.dolifedifferent.org.

Do Life Different

Doing it different: Look back to a time of struggle. Identify three blessings that came out of it. How can you apply that realization to your current and future struggles?

_____

_____

_____

_____

_____

_____

_____

_____

_____

_____

_____

_____

_____

_____

49. are you using what God gave you?

"I tell you that to everyone who has, more will be given, but as for the one who has nothing, even what they have will be taken away." Luke 19:26 NIV

Jesus tells Parable of the Ten Minas found in Luke 19:11-27 about a nobleman and his ten servants. The nobleman is going on a trip and gives each of his ten servants a mina. He leaves them with the instructions to put the money to good use until he returns.

While he is gone, the servants take very different approaches to handling the money, each knowing they'll have to report when he returns. When the day of his return arrives, he calls the servants to give an account.

The first servant tells his master he's increased what was given to him and earned an additional ten minas. The nobleman is very pleased and gives him charge over ten cities. The next servant has earned five minas, so is given five cities to govern.

Do Life Different

The next servant cowers before the nobleman, explaining he was afraid. He hid the mina to ensure he could return it untouched. The nobleman is angry with this servant. He should have at least put the money in the bank and earned interest. He gives this servant's mina to the one who earned ten.

This parable has a strong message for us. It challenges us to ask how we're handling what God has entrusted to us. What resources has God blessed you with? Think of not just business resources, but time with children, local church, and neighbors.

Are we using these wisely? Or squandering time and money on things that make *us* happy?

When we look through the lens of stewardship, we can see whether we're good stewards of all God has given. We must be diligent to focus on stewardship, so we don't get to the end of our lives having hidden the resources because we, like the servant, were too afraid to use them.

Video devo 49 is available at www.dolifedifferent.org.

Jill Hart

Doing it different: Are you a faithful steward of the resources God has given you? Are there areas in your life that could improve?

Do Life Different

50. success without pain?

David fought them from dusk until the evening of the next day, and none of them got away, except four hundred young men who rode off on camels and fled.
1 Samuel 30:17 NIV

In 1 Samuel 30, David returns home from marching with King Achish to find his town burned and the women and children taken captive. He asks God if he can pursue the raiding party and God says yes, chase them and you will succeed.

Notice what comes next in the passage. As David and his army set off to pursue the enemies that have their wives and children, 200 of the men are *"too exhausted to cross the valley" (v 10)*. They've just come from a long journey and are worn out.

The rest of the men, while tired, continue to ride on with David. They reach the enemy and then fight *"from dusk until the evening of the next day."* Twenty-four hours straight. They succeed, but there is an incredible amount of determination, perseverance, and work involved.

Even though God tells them they will succeed, they have to do the work, fight the fight. God assured them ultimate victory, not an easy win.

Their success certainly wasn't easy. There were likely times when they questioned whether they would succeed, even though God had said they would. Just because He says something will happen doesn't mean it will come to us easily.

This holds true for us as well. When God calls us to a task, we often expect that task to be easy. After all, if God asked, surely all will fall into place seamlessly, right? Sometimes it does work this way. Several battles in the Old Testament God confused the enemy and they ran away.

However, more often than not, the battle must be fought in order to gain the victory. Beth Moore states, "God often gives us victory that requires blood, sweat, and tears. By doing this He is strengthening us and maturing us in the process."

The battle is worth the effort, not just because we gain victory, but because of the refining that is done in the process. Whether it's the battle of building a

Do Life Different

business, or of raising a family, or of keeping our marriage together – the battle is worth it.

Video devo 50 is available at www.dolifedifferent.org.

Doing it different: What battle are you facing? How can you show up to the battle each day, ready to learn and eager to grow? How can you encourage a battle weary friend?

_____
_____
_____
_____
_____
_____
_____
_____
_____
_____

Jill Hart

51. that pesky step of faith

> *So Abram went, as the Lord had told him; and Lot went with him. Abram was seventy-five years old when he set out from Harran. Genesis 12:4 NIV*

What step of faith have you turned away from? What are you're holding yourself back from doing?

When I quit my job and started working from home, I had no idea what I was doing or what to expect. I'm not sure what made me think I could make this working from home thing a viable system that would thrive and provide for my family. Where did I get the courage?

I made so little money with my first at-home job it's laughable. There were lots of sacrifices in those days. We went down to one car. We ate at home. We scrimped and saved and barely scraped by. This isn't a get-your-cake-and-eat-it-too lifestyle. It's not for the faint of heart. It's hard work and determination.

Do Life Different

Yet, somehow, with the Holy Spirit's help, I felt compelled to take this step of faith and go for it. I felt God asking me to trust Him with our finances and with how it'd all work out. It took faith to quit my job, and starting CWAHM was another step of faith. And I continue to take steps of faith all these years later.

Each person who lived God's way in Scripture displayed intense trust in Him. Many times more than just faith – action was required.

In Abram's case, God said *go* and so he did. Abram didn't fuss or fight. He simply went.

It's never quite that easy for me. I fret and worry and question God about what He's asked.

Do you struggle in this area? Or are you quick to do as God asks of you?

Abram picked up his family and moved when God asked. We're told later in Abram's story that his faith was credited to him as righteousness. It wasn't his actions that saved him. It was his faith. God eventually rewards Abram's faith by changing his name to Abraham and making him the "father of many nations."

We'll be asked to take steps of faith often when we follow God. Let's take a cue from Abraham and walk forward, trusting God.

Jill Hart

Video devo 51 is available at www.dolifedifferent.org.

Doing it different: How can you emulate the faith and trust of Abram? How can you model it for your children?

_____
_____
_____
_____
_____
_____
_____
_____
_____
_____
_____
_____
_____

52. make your life count

Why, you do not even know what will happen tomorrow. What is your life? You are a mist that appears for a little while and then vanishes. James 4:14 NIV

Genesis 5 lists a genealogy stretching from Adam to Noah. Within this genealogy of men (and a few women) many lived over 800 years. Can you imagine living that long?

Despite that longevity, many have just one short line of Scripture attributed to their lives. Hundreds of years, but they're a tiny blip on God's timeline.

What will God say about our lives? We might make it to 90 or 100 years old. How will we have filled that blip?

I want my blip to count.

A friend of mine had a work-at-home idea. She was really excited, but worried about starting something while her kids were small and still at home with her. She asked me if I thought that by working from home with small kids she would be taking away from their childhood in some way.

Rarely does God ask me to do something when it's convenient for me. I encouraged her to pray over it, talk with her husband, and be sure what God was asking of her. And if it was, then she could step forward confident God had not only her needs, but the needs of kids under control.

We are not guaranteed tomorrow. If God asks us to do something, we need to do it, trusting God along the way.

James 4:14 gives us some hard words to digest, *"What is your life? You are a mist that appears for a little while and then vanishes."*

We do not have forever. Our blip can end at any time.

Today is the day to do what God asks. Start a business. Step out in ministry. Meet your neighbors. Whatever it is, do it.

Make your blip count.

Video devo 52 is available at www.dolifedifferent.org.

Do Life Different

Doing it different: Do you need a mentor, coach, or more education to move forward? Do you need a prayer partner? Or do you just need to walk in faith?

Jill Hart's entrepreneurial career began in her teens when she spent a summer helping her father with his vending business, stocking pop and candy machines. When he put her in charge of a Coke machine and let her keep the profits, she saw the benefits of being her own boss.

That entrepreneurial spirit motivates her to show other women how to begin and build their own businesses from home. Jill is the founder of the popular Christian work-at-home website, CWAHM.com, reaching thousands of women each month.

Jill writes, speaks, and counsels others about finding a business niche and balance while working from home. She also co-authored *So You Want To Be a Work-at-Home Mom*. Jill presents hope for moms who desire to be at home with their children and encourages women to experience our extraordinary God in everyday life. Jill lives in Nebraska with her husband and two kids and works in her pajamas as often as possible.

Christian Work at Home Ministries started in the year 2000 based on a simple premise: Jill Hart wanted to reach out to other moms working from home. She imagined that it would be a fun hobby and something to fill her time. She had no idea what God had planned. Since then, CWAHM has grown into a powerhouse organization consisting of a community of literally thousands of members. From those who dream of starting their own work-at-home careers, to those who already own home-based businesses, CWAHM offers support and encouragement no matter where they are on their journey.

CWAHM provides job listings, encouragement, classified ads, expert information, and most of all, community. At CWAHM.com you'll find all you need to start, maintain, and grow your work-at-home business. Visit www.cwahm.com today and find out how you can make your work-at-home dream a reality.

Do Life Different

Electric Moon Publishing, LLC offers collaborative publishing services for the indie author, ministry, business, and organization. We assist authors with editing and writing, cover design and interior layout, paperback/hardback printing, and marketing/distribution.

For more information, contact us at
info@emoonpublishing.com
or
www.emoonpublishing.com.

www.ingramcontent.com/pod-product-compliance
Lightning Source LLC
Chambersburg PA
CBHW061324040426
42444CB00011B/2766